The Last Time I Saw You

PRAISE FOR *THE LAST TIME I SAW YOU*

'Akhil Katyal is a gifted poet with a remarkable imagination, capturing the intricate intellectual and emotional complexities of experience. It's incredible how language takes shape in his hands, effortlessly breaking archetypes one after another. The intensity with which he confronts grief and separation is so palpable that it feels impossible to escape.' – VIVEK SHANBHAG

'A poet of traces and silhouettes margined by light. Of promises and hopes lined with a growing dark. Of love and longing and love's likelihood in a land where each one is a city of their own wounds. Where saints can come only to die. A poet who sings of life's eternal grief, sadness, and pain in stunning metaphors, similes, and imagery. Always serene. A maverick you will adore.' – GEETANJALI SHREE

'Akhil Katyal becomes ever more lyrical with every gentle evocation of people and places that are no longer his. In these poems of love and longing, the gossamer filter of his loss colours the world differently but reveals that absence itself is rich and full and suffused with its own aching beauty.' – ARSHIA SATTAR

'Visceral and soft, this book is a greening, and the promise of a greening. You move from poem to poem, following grief and love from cityscape to stolen moment to acute pain of memory: Akhil Katyal's words move you deftly through the land and her languages, carrying a steady diet of devotion, bereavement and balm. It pulled bismillahs from me all along and is a beautiful reminder: poets grow wild and irrepressible in our shared land.' – KYLA PASHA

'Akhil Katyal's poetry is an allegory of urban middle-class life. His poetic sensibility emerges from ordinary, everyday existence, from both its celebrations and struggles. His poems supplement the readers' world of feelings in such a way that they feel, in poem after poem, that their own memories are being rekindled. In his work, Delhi is the key metaphor, one in which he lives and one which he is in constant search of.' – ADNAN KAFEEL 'DARWESH'

The Last Time I Saw You

poems

AKHIL KATYAL

HarperCollins *Publishers* India

First published in India by HarperCollins *Publishers* 2024
4th Floor, Tower A, Building No. 10, DLF Cyber City,
DLF Phase II, Gurugram, Haryana – 122002
www.harpercollins.co.in

2 4 6 8 10 9 7 5 3 1

Copyright © Akhil Katyal 2024

P-ISBN: 978-93-6213-462-2
E-ISBN: 978-93-6213-856-9

Akhil Katyal asserts the moral right
to be identified as the author of this work.

All rights reserved. No part of this publication may be reproduced,
stored in a retrieval system, or transmitted, in any form or by any means,
electronic, mechanical, photocopying, recording or otherwise,
without the prior permission of the publishers.

Typeset in 12/16 Arno Pro at
HarperCollins *Publishers* India

Printed and bound in India by
Manipal Technologies Limited

This book is produced from independently certified FSC® paper to ensure
responsible forest management.

for G
who might not read this

It had occurred to me that all human beings are divided
into those who wish to move forward
and those who wish to go back.
Or you could say, those who wish to keep moving
and those who want to be stopped in their tracks
as by the blazing sword.

LOUISE GLÜCK

CONTENTS

ETYMOLOGY

Grief comes from *grever*, burden, the weight you carry, the holding on to land beneath your feet, unmistakable like its kin, *gravity*. Sadness comes from the old *sæd*, sated, weary, the sense of the last hour, the wilting of mountain grass, the unexpected density of stars, the restlessness of your head on the arms of enough. Pain comes from *poena*, *punish*, a shrinking of the sun, long corridors of wall and metal and a slow unknowing of mercy, an unknowing of what to do with a sudden expansion of time, a traffic of remembering. You left and the sentence does not end

TWELVE VARIATIONS ON A SOBTI LINE

इतना बारीक न सूतिये कि हमारी जान पर बन आए
اتنا باریک نہ سوتیے کہ ہماری جان پر بن آئے

Krishna Sobti

Do not thresh me so thin that I die.
Do not cut me so sharp that I break.
Do not braid me so fine that I sigh.
Do not shear me so close that I ache.
Do not press me so hard that I paper.
Do not knit me so tight that I tear.
Do not sear me so far that I vapour.
Do not draw me so red that I scare.
Do not crush me so muslin that I fly.
Do not burn me so ash that I winter.
Do not spin me so cunning that I cry.
Do not shard me so hot that I splinter.

IT CAN EXTINGUISH EVEN A WILDFIRE

It can pull a recalcitrant planet closer.

It can make a day pass
without the necessary rituals
of hand-wringing and retrospection.

It can fall, like rain,
on sunburnt quartzite.

It can make the three poets I read
this week – one, a curly-haired eschatologist,
another, a dirge-singer by the sea, and
the third, a silhouette of a man –
seem a little less lonely.

It can dwell in any word
in the dictionary, even
in *gloaming*. Or in
the etymology of *bereaves.*

It can fall out, unexpectedly,
from an old notebook (presumed
lost) from the page I had once used
to show you what it looked like
in Nastaliq.

Now I find that it, too,
can dry up like old leaves.

Your name.

THE WARBLER TENDS TO

the cuckoo's egg.

If only it had known.

When you went away
you left me nothing.

I raised it like my own.

I COME BACK TO MY FLAT

In the living room
you're sitting on the landlord's sofa
tying your shoelaces.

In the study, I am
pulling you behind the shelves
for one more kiss.

In the kitchen, you're putting
the three extra spoons of sugar
in your morning tea.

At the washbasin,
naked, you're cleaning up
the mess we've made.

In the bedroom, you're
sitting up on my side of the bed,
your back reticent.

In each place
you're always there.

In each place,
you're readying
to leave.

USTAD BISMILLAH KHAN

Once, to an interviewer,
he held up his right palm
and in the way his fingers stood,
he found alif, he found laam,
till he could read the name of God.

After such revelation,
what could his instrument do
if not consecrate
every sky it touched.

The last time I heard him,
he had turned each grain of wood
in his shehnai into a riverside,
each breath into a stunning desolation.

What could a child born in the middle
of a war promise his world, except
that there is no faith bigger
than the octave.

I heard, as if sitting on 'the last ghat'
in his city, his final note, so long and
so inconsolable, it could hold us all.

NIGHT SOUNDS AT SAFDARJUNG TOMB

عزیز! اب میں اڑتے پتّوں کا ماتم دار ہوں
अज़ीज़! अब मैं उड़ते पत्तों का मातमदार हूँ।
... now I am the mourner for drifting leaves.
Intizar Hussain

The poetry of earth is ceasing never.
John Keats

The rasp of the jhingurs scraping
their forewings behind the hibiscus.
The floating arguments of the mynas

returning to their nests. The prowling
echoes of the skelter bats. The headlit
horns whetted by a red signal outside.

The alert clicks of a camera in the small
hands of a curly-haired novice. His 'Chalein?'
to a friend when they're done. The shuffle

of their feet on old gravel. The footsteps
of the short guard minding the stanchions,
keeping a stray couple from the night.

A parrot's drop, light as a kerchief, in the hauz,
the sandstone of the tomb suddenly rippled.
The quiet press of a band of pigeons on the

dome drawn by an expert Abyssinian hand.
The guards discussing their change of duties
The anomalous graze of a landing on a nearby

airstrip. Under the rococo sky, the disturbed
sleep of the Wazir ul-Mamlak-i-Hindustan.
On my shoulder, the thin crush of your whisper.

DAY ONE OF LEARNING ITALIAN

Before we learn the verbs for *eating*
or *drinking*, or the nouns for *bread*

and *water*, we are taught the words
for *man* and *woman*, *girl* and *boy*,

as if those are the survival skills
for the first day in a new country.

We step into a new language
through the customs desk of

gender. I don't yet know how
to ask a pretty stranger for an

address, or request bartenders
for a glass of water (or a beer)

– all useful skills, mind you, as
first days go. All I know is to show

off my *ragazza* and *ragazzo*, *la donna*
and *l'uomo*. What is the need of

learning a new language if you
only confirm bits of plastic scenery

you thought you'd left behind? What
is the need to travel five and a half

seas to find new nouns for old things?
The teacher is impassive – 'Why expect

a language to be kind on its first day?
Why make it into a djinn?' It doesn't

live to answer some simple wish, it won't
allow you to step out of everything.

FOR G, ONE EVENING RETURNED FROM WORK

Is there anything more beautiful
than helmet-pressed hair? Once it's off,
his forehead is such a snack. I could
munch down that black confection
falling over his eyes, those thumb-pressed
curls, that yummm sort-of-waviness.

The little crushes in his hair tell me
this dude is a dude-about-town. Wears
his sweat and dust, his motorcycle
sort of musk like a grungy crown.
Street-smart, worldly-wise, safe-when-he-
has-to-be, stunt-man-on-his-off-days, come on,
lay him out on a pan and feed the needy.

Touch his hair, climb those steps, reach
the highs, that boyishness that unmade hair
gives him is let's-not-mince-words paradise.
So beer-drink him. Seat him. Greet him.
Then eat him. Glass-clink him. Choc-lick him.
Try him. Pry him. Open. Hair-flick him. Down-
dick him. Let him rest. Then lip-stick him. Thigh
him. Dry him. Sleep. Next day, pillion-ride & fly him.

DARWIN

noted a furrowing of the forehead and
an 'obliquity of the eyebrows' caused by

two separate conditions, one, the influence
of grief, and two, when staring at the sun.

He even made three of his children 'look as long
and as attentively' at a needle-tip of a redwood

against a scorched sky to make his case. In all
three, he saw the 'grief-muscles' contracting.

Grief-muscles: how strange to turn the long arrears
of sorrow into small bundles of fibrous tissue,

the passion of Christ into a materialist consolation.
There must surely be a secret search for respite in

locating the cause of grief in the same place as the
source of light, to read in the lines of a troubled

forehead an insistence that, when it reaches flesh,
your touch and the sun are indistinguishable.

I TRANSLATE YOUR NAME INTO NINE LANGUAGES

and read each shape as a warning sign

In Armenian
the second letter is a U-turn.

In Hebrew, your name halts
for breath.

In Malayalam, the heart
wears a cap, sits on its bum.

In Uzbek, you open
in a rounder vowel,
need more work.

In Somali, you keep mum,
close yourself off
at each end.

You fall with an unexpected
thud in Gurmukhi.

In Odia (look at you!)
you're too smooth
to care.

In Japanese (like always)
you're separated by air.

GOD HASN'T ABANDONED YOU

He has, instead,
by evidence of empty buildings
near railway tracks

ABUNDONED
ABONDED
ABBADONED

His complete forsaking
always misses the mark.

Instead, rooms are painted
by half consolations,
trust is hung on walls
like old calendars, old chairs
are lived in by late replies,
floors swept weekly
by one-tenth of a promise
and windowpanes broken
in the shape of an explanation.

Between his final leaving
and you

        always
a letter or two.

with thanks to Eunice de Souza

READING *JEJURI* ON MY WAY TO THE 9 A.M. CLASS

after a night of rainstorms

You wake up
to fallen trees

'Half the routes are blocked,'
the auto guy lets off steam

near Nizamuddin,
he heard, a bus was flattened
under a peepul

all your way, branches,
wind-amputated

on the road
a sudden loss of nests

a black kite
looking for a home
swoops down in a line
of Kolatkar.

I SHUT MY EYES

from the blistering sun

but it remains etched
on the eyelid

a small, bare silhouette
margined by light

a trace not allowed
to leave.

Every time you leave,
I shut my eyes.

HANERI

In Lucknow
when we were young
Ma would use this word to describe
those evenings that were quilted
with the thick colour
of dust.

As the wind quickened
around our elbows

the sky
turned red
then bronze, then rust

soon, raised like
an army of mercenaries
from the ground, sand,
in great torrents
whiplashing
our sleeves

till clusters of children
formed in the evening fields
beside the colony homes
were all summarily called back

because
haneri aa rahi hai.

Its arrival
stunningly transcribed
in the skies.

Sometimes, the dust storm
was so thick, we felt
we were thickening
into a giant ball
of wool.

Too young then
to know the lesson
in the word

too full
of ourselves
to know things that
somehow carried in their own names
their consequence:

hanera is dark
haneri, then, would turn the edges
of the skies, almost viscous,
into the primitive colour
of congealing
blood

the sheets of sand
– hurricaned from their home –
cut the asphalt

as we ran back
to our homes.

We never learnt
to pick up the signs
of impending storms.

Even though
in years to come
people would enter
our lives, saying, early on,
strange, confusing, wonderful things
– airlifting us in their breeze –
they would, if only we heard
closely enough, line
their promises with
a growing dark

but we did not listen

we did not mark
the colours of the skies
like a giant palm
waiting to be read by us.

We did not
see it coming

as the blood of
their early promise

veined across our days
and our dreams

slowed, lay still
around us

in reams
and reams

something in
them revealing

their promise

molecule
by molecule

congealing.

ORDINARY THINGS

Doorbells rang.
Scripts were graded.
Parents called.

Last week
the nasturtium survived
a sudden relocation
into an older flowerpot,
its miniature hats
still holding
dew.

On Tuesday,
a paper sent their photographer.
He was trained well,
every few minutes,
to put me at ease
he said 'You have a nice smile'
or 'You have very interesting features'.
Even his lies were restrained,
neutral, could go either way.
Like when teachers say 'interesting'
to a colleague's remark,
he offered only non-committal compliments.

In the crossword last morning,
9 down was a five-letter word,
a synonym for short-lived.

The plumber came
and I couldn't finish the game.

He mended the taps.
Standing next to him,
I overcooked the rice.
The paper lay quietly.

9 across
was your name.

He left, I ate what I'd made,
called my mother, took the clothes
off the line.

All the time
we knew each other,
your lies were always restrained,
neutral, could go either way.

Now, like winter flowers,
I am to survive a sudden relocation.

On the balcony,
the last of the evening's sun
does its stunt
then through the night
grief, like a well-fed lion,
sits next to me, rests,
doesn't need to hunt.

with thanks to Zehra Nigah

SANJAY VAN

At one point, there were so many butterflies,
we were afraid of stepping on one. Imagine

the boot's sudden crush on the thin chintz of
a wing, the losing of a life at such a small scale

only the grain of the quartzite could hear it.
My friend tells me how the Aravallis were

born. The crystalline stone – an old witness
to a continent crumpling like paper to make our

home – now listening, intently, to the smallest
account of what makes all our living possible,

each day, without knowing, astray, a crushing
of something beautiful, then a turning away.

DAY ELEVEN OF LEARNING ITALIAN

Suddenly a word
so light, so like
what it means

its sound
turns the tongue
into the thing it describes

say it and the word
draws its wings
and flies

off the page
like a little
farfalla.

SCRABBLE

If you have the letters E X P E C T A T I O N
you could make 'excite'
or, better advised, 'patience'
or last resort, 'panic'
(all along 'toxic' is an option).

If you have the letters R E P L Y
you could hope for 'rely'
or else, 'yelp',
if nothing comes
ask for help.

If you have the letters D E S I R E
in the middle of that growing
fire, it always 'rides'
– every time you take his name –
but if the embers cool
then it lets up, 'dries',
and if you've been a fool,
then someday, somewhere
without you
knowing,
'dies'.

NICKNAME

Two vowels,
three consonants.

A gift you had plucked
from the language of infants
and given to me

mid-conversation
while asking for a glass of water.

It had surprised me the first time
but, in days, I let the sound
hang in the room
like an unexpected
fallen eyelash.

When you weren't around,
I kept it on the edge
of my knuckles

with two friends,
belief and air.

You used to say it
like a daily spell,
sometimes compressed
to a thin cloth of decibels

when you kept it like a whisper
on my pillow.

Almost asleep,
once, you exhaled the word.

In an unexpected argument, one day,
I got caught in the elegant Garamond
of the way you said it.

It has been a year
since I heard it.

All my attempts to calculate
the power it still has,
and then work backwards,
always fail.

Padel calls this period of the long after
'the safety of not / being loved'.
The memory of the sound
finds a rent in its thin quilt, steps in.

It is a difficult gift
when I see it now
in the stained glass of years.

It always did
what a pet name promised.

To willingly reduce us
in the intimacy of others.

To touch us
like some ancient
pat on the head,
like a need we would not admit.

To show us the map
to a future we pluck
from the language
of unheeding stars.

To give us
the promise of gold.

As the sun goes down,
leading the fox, lost
in the white vast of the tundra,
to the leghold.

A PAINTER ONCE TOLD ME

'The hardest to draw
is the hand.'

The most accomplished ones
falter, give their sitters
swollen knuckles, spidery fingers
or a wrist that looks like
it would never turn.

While the eyes burn
with longing or a well-hidden sadness,
the hands refuse to believe
their story.

The thumb sometimes leaves
the other fingers in a huff,
or the phalanges are too rough
and the joints are often in places
where, if they were to really be,
they would always ache.

I asked her why this is so.

She replied, displaying her own
as some sort of proud specimen:
'How could that be perfect
from which we give and take.'

THE MARIGOLD FIELDS OF BURARI

All through the sunlit
stretch of the Bund Road
couples have parked their bikes.

They have carved
these secret spots on the roadside
merely by being here.

It does not matter
if it is the middle of the day
and the sun is shining on them
and everyone passing by can see.

They are far away from their homes
and have draped themselves
in that magic distance.

They don't need, like once
in another city I had seen,
on the wave breakers by the sea,
the small excuses of handkerchiefs
or umbrellas or dupattas to draw
a charmed circle around them.

They are here, against
the March crop of marigolds
growing behind their backs,
streaking the banks of the Jamuna
with sunspots.

The bank of the Jamuna
is not their school, or mohalla,
or the furthest distance
their fathers can see.

On my way back,
motorcycles laden with sacks
of marigolds are already on their way
to the Ghazipur phool mandi.

They will take these flowers to the temples

and the rushed longing
of these boys and girls
will become prayers
in other hands.

AFTER MAIDAN GARHI

everyone grows thorns
to protect themselves.

Under your feet
the stones
are no longer stones
but foothills

land is
unintended cricket fields
then dust
then leopard pugmarks.

This is the desert
signing you in

slowly
through kikar's checkpost.

They call it the devil tree
they call it the mad one
vilayati kikar.

It asks you for water.

The British brought it from Mexico
to Delhi in the 1920s,
making a mistake the size of kings.

It choked all trees around it
it stole their water.

I walk cautiously in its dust
mindful of geckos

find a tree
the size of my mistakes

leave your memory
on a low branch.

A slow wind
lifts the dust on its arms.

As I return
groundwater recedes

further
and then further.

A SECOND IS < A MINUTE

a minute is < a day
a day is < a month
& so on & up & away
till lustrums & decades & jubilees
& centuries cross our way
to a millennium which is < an aeon
which is < what I'm trying to say
i.e. add them all together
units big & small
their sum will still be smaller
than waiting for your call

THE ROOM BECAME ORDINARY AGAIN

the night you left.

It returned
to its straight-backed walls
and its small doors.

The floor somehow
was stone again

and the one window
that looked out
turned into the grain
of waiting.

As the sacrament
of your voice slowly left
the doorstep

everything that had
been briefly mystified
by a strange hand
returned to this world.

When I came back
to my room knowing
it no longer housed miracles,
that you were no longer mine

I could feel the body
of every thing turn
into bread, the blood
of every hour turn
into wine.

AS A UNIT OF MEASUREMENT

kos
(from *krośa,* 'call')
was the distance
at which another human
could be heard.

I didn't know
distance could be measured
in decibels.

Counting how far
a call carries seems like
measuring the world
in units of longing.

Koson dur.

Each complete
only when
a voice fades.

These days
you stand always
on that side of the kos.

In a place
where my voice loses
even to air.

TYPES OF FALLING

A coin drops into the pocket.
A leaf slows to the ground.
An eagle nosedives to its prey.
The passer-by trips on the curb.
An egg is dislodged from the nest.
The graph dips for a day.
The night sinks behind the window.
Silence descends like a Mary Oliver poem.
Your hand slips down the waist.
I move towards you and call it falling.

THERE'S SOMETHING WRONG

with my doorbell.

Whenever it rains
it starts ringing on its own.

Once at midnight
the plastic birdsong
filled my apartment
and I woke up to no one.

The next morning
the electrician told me
that water seeps
into the wiring
setting off conduction.

I nodded and paid
for the repair.

The rain was at my door
and I did not answer.

I WISH THERE WAS A WAY TO DOWNLOAD OUR DREAMS

into easy MP4s.
Play them on a loop.
Try and make sense.

What did D mean when he said,
sitting in three cabs at once:
'That's the trouble with you lot
who don't get angry at your exes.'

Behind him,
a film playing.
Audrey Hepburn and
Kunal Khemu (yes) and in scene
after scene, Audrey repeating a line:
'Your cruelty is so laid-back.'

And what is Ma'am Adams
from school doing here?
Why is she swallowing a noon ghunna?
She wasn't ever nasal
in her geography classes
as she pointed out the Euphrates
or Lake Tanganyika.

In my dream, I try
to get angry at you.

Three tributaries
sprout from my hands.

In my dream,
Ma'am Adams is talking of
all the water that the Euphrates carried.

Three tributaries
in a horizon of sands.
An old river
fighting a desert

like a tongue
fights a new language.

You are nowhere,
nowhere near.

Someone in the dream says:
'I hold you responsible
for the bareness of my days.'

When I wake up
I am eating the words.

FIRST DAYS

I was to make a home
in your touch.

I was to make a home
in make-believe.

Can you pick me up
some bread and milk?

– the first time you
came over to mine

I already asked of you
a dailiness. That night

your fingers were
a well-told lie. That night

a tincture of hope and
madness. In the years

since, I have asked:
What could you have done

to persuade me of love's
likelihood? That first night,

the chips were already
falling like a Tetris game

the carbon sky was allotting
its honour and blame. Next

to you, I turned the lights
off. The room was agnostic.

When I tried to sleep, you
quietened the city for me.

EACH NIGHT

I go to sleep with thoughts
of walking in another city.
As the heartbeat slows down
I turn into unfamiliar streets.

Breathing slower, I begin to
belong to another air, another
water. I am strolling through
Lucknow, Karachi, Lagos and

the moon is drifting away from
the earth at one point five inches
a year. I am walking in a different
aabo-hawa, Seattle, Agra, Jhang

as sleep is beginning to spindle
around my feet. I dream-meet
old friends, sometimes a day old,
sometimes a decade, chatting,

hanging around corners, as if they
always knew each other. As if there
is a place, other than the funeral,
where everyone you have ever

known goes to meet. They show
each other the cities of their wounds
as I sink deeper and deeper into
the limestone of the night. In my

dream, someone says the word for
'lost' in their language and it sounds
like 'person'. Do not wait if you see
me sleeping. Tell me which way.

A SAINT CAME TO DIE IN OUR LAND

I keep telling G
I will peak at forty.

He doesn't believe me.

In the afternoon
we leave the marble tomb
behind us, its white
blistering in the sun.

G says, 'Can you stop
the sun for me?'

My father notes down
his favourite couplets in a notebook
smaller than my palm.

He would have copied
out G's line.

All of childhood we were told
there would be a school trip
to the marble tomb.

It never happened.

But we did not learn
to not look for peaks
in the small orbits of our lives.

As kids, we knew that ‘wonder’
lay under that white dome.

Our plans were made
of outside food, living
next door, trump cards and
claims chalked out in little corridors.

The first time I saw the marble tomb
– years later, a friend drove us –
I did not believe there could be
such a white in the world.

We asked the guide to explain it.

Kaifi said, ‘Doodh ki nahar mein
jis tarah ubaal aa jaaye.’

The marmar translated, as if
‘a stream of milk had suddenly
come to a boil’.

When I say I will peak at forty
I mean to abdicate the failures
of so far, to augur my way
to where the railway tracks meet.

In the cab, the breeze
fills up our masks, while I hold
the future to ransom.

I keep telling G I will peak
at that age far enough to make
see-saw promises about.

He replies like a general
negotiating terms of surrender.

No word amenable
to further digging or discovery.

As if his sound
was its own meaning
needing no separate parsing
or prophecy.

Some sounds need no parsing.
They are their own prophecy.

The year Bismillah Khan died
I was in Malkaganj, sitting under
the clock tower.

In the crowd, I could not distinguish
the passing of an age.

In every palm, they held
large crescents of jaggery,
martbaans of trapped songs
and a piece of an irreversible world.

When G left,
it was that two score again.
The future is always
more reliable than what we hold
in our inept hands.

I wish I hadn't made claims
he could keep
in his pocket
and leave.

There are so many kinds
of leavings, some which can
flower an entire people

in another land, where slowly
the fingers of their arrival
grow, and their jasper hearts,
and some which leave a rock
silence in their wake.

Once, a friend
told me about a saint
who walked many hundreds of miles
to come and die
in the town where I was born

only so that people
may make wishes
by the edge of his tomb

tie threads on a window
trellised with wishes

in each twist
a promised son or daughter
a lover's return
a pay raise, or the early death
of an abhorrent in-law.

When he passed,
he'd already done the penance,
sung the dirge

and performed the miracle
that made this fallow piece of land
a durbar of an eccentric
and generous king

who could grant you
anything, if only you opened
your hands in a surrender
underwritten by faith.

His resting place
yielded desires like a desert,
in each shrub, a promise of water.

By his head
lay a granite mortar
filled with salt,
that once tasted,
could cure all illnesses.

When my people came
– G did not say *your*
people – axe in hand,
to demolish this shrine,
they knew their
thirst was girded
by a common silence.

They want to open the basement rooms
of the marble tomb. They say
they will find our gods.

I don't want anything to do with gods
for whom the dead have to be disturbed.

Will the firoza in our eyes outlive
the animus of our hands?

I don't want anything to do with gods
for whom they stalk the street
like a pall, spreading.

Will the sulaimani in our hands
survive the haneri of their eyes?

They are still your gods
whether you like them or not.

The guide told us nothing
of how the stone turns into papier mâché.

You cannot go on abdicating gods
like this, not owning up to their failures.

In the notebook smaller than my palm,
my father notes down a line

of sight that goes straight
to the finial.

We peak together,
if some of us are not
thrown down

if some of us do not learn
– not every discovery
is a form of growing.

Manucci tells me
'in the foundations'
of my city were ordered
'several decapitated criminals
to be placed as a sign of sacrifice'.

Doubt the motivations
of those who go looking
for gods with a shovel.

Who don't know
how to mark us out
from the age of empires.

To let the dead sleep
is a learned art.

To become literate
in living next door.

Own up to the gods you were born to,
don't mitigate the image of their poison,
find antidotes to their sting.

In front of you, a people
are being turned
into a foil.

No use telling them
you don't believe in the gods
stitched to your name.

We will have no one
to give this world to.

No one except the river
to carry our dead.

We don't peak in an imagined dawn.
We have no beginnings
like the day's first prayers.

We will only dig the ground
and find what we already know:
our animus made into a god.

When you left, G, I asked
every part of my city
to yield all its memories,
entered them in a register
so that no one would say
they weren't there.

In *Ankahi,* made before
I was born, the little boy
with a hole in his heart
speaks only in aphorisms:
Baaji, aap zindagi ko
kya samajhti hain?
Jibran kahta hai
zindagi milne, aur phir
judaa ho jaane, aur phir
mil jaane ke amal ko kahte hain.

With a shovel, I thought
I could go looking for assurance
of having been loved.

The last generation is too eager
to pass this world into our hands.

They make it sound like a gift.

To let go of the past is a learned art.
To not go digging for something
to plot its spurious return.

To understand
the passing of an age
allows us to live in the coral
of the present.

Every ground is sacred.

We should let gods remain.

We should not sieve
the dust of the Jamuna for anklets.

My people must not look
for a sleeping god
under the doorsteps
of the living.

We should not keep our hands
on every stone and
claim it for ourselves.

There is god within the rooms
of our miserable hearts.

We should not seek him
in the agate of our neighbour's sleep.

THE DOORBELL BREAKS THE DREAM

just as you are about to step
into my room. I open
the door.

A dream
breaks
into my room.

WRITE A POEM WITHOUT TIME

The problem begins in the title,
the damn verb ('write') ushers in action,
action ushers in time.

Try again.
(Meanwhile, verbs keep sneaking in.)

Perhaps only nouns, suspended
outside all hours, like: a black drongo,
an underlit swimming pool,
a jacaranda tree.

A refusal of time is a refusal
of memory. Like: a startling place,
like: that night. A button moon
stitched to the sky like a plea.

Here the black drongo will not
dive from the elbowed branch
of the small jacaranda
into the wavering light
of the pool.

It will not wet its feathers
in the brilliant school of water.

It will not reference
any past, will not hold
onto reluctant debris.

It will be weightless.

It will not script
your impossible return
in the sudden refraction
of this night of after.

THE FORK IN THE ROAD IS A MYTH

In life, when you turn,
at least seventeen paths
face you

in each, a twilight
walks backwards.

The French chose
a strange word
for 'man'.

It sounds
as if he's always
in an afterthought
– ummm

as if weighing
an invisible scale
at the precise moment
God names him

homme.

Language, confidante,
keeps everything
we scuttle

as we keep living
in our favourite self-image
– of having to choose
between seventeen ways
of being arranged
on a crucifix.

YOUR ROOM, LATE WINTER

the quilt, cannablissed,
the bedsheet, wronged
into mogras, the curtains,
assailed – as you drew them –
in a sudden flight of snapdragons.

And you, slowly, tendrilled around me.

I THROW OPEN THE NEW

bedsheet – a sudden slow
of yellow and green in my
hands – spring beginning
unexpectedly in the vortex
of my room, a quick rush
in the head, sunlit pleats
with hints of new leaves,
airborne like whispers of
a prairie, 'a thing of beauty'
is also a thing of fear, out
of the blue, a glimpse of
the last year, of what could
have been between me and
you, the sides of the small
bed holding extinct birds
briefly come back to life,
all the residue, intrusions
of a possibility, a suspicion
climbing the low wooden
frame till I tuck it under the
rock of the mattress. How
unready for happiness to be
this afraid of sudden colour.

AN INVENTED MEMORY

As the Ravi
crosses Khokhar Town
the sun sets
into a Ferris wheel.

The city still
remembers to leave
three small hands
of furrowed green
between the riverbank
and the clamouring brown
of the last houses.

Above you, the sky
is in the throes of cirrus.

Below, the blackening water
refuses to wash away our sins.

Behind, in a smog outline,
the minarets of Badshahi
keep a slow count
of the years we spent
to find the sudden solace
of each other.

WHEN THE NIGHT MARKET AT BHOGAL CLOSES

it is as if

I fold back the pillow cushions,
wrap up the bed sheets, the ear
rings, the Q-tips, roll back the
socks with lily prints and Winnie-
the-Poohs and tulips, order the
last chai, closely spoon the bra
cups into one another, put the
pickles back in the jar, cram the
plastic mirrors into big brown
boxes & the buckets, the knives,
the bath mugs back in their cello-
phanes, the goldfish in the bowls,
wall clocks in cotton folds, lidded,
scissor packets, debts acquitted,
I say my goodbyes, find an auto
to load the stuff, see what's done
today, and tomorrow, what is due,
think of dinner, then, think of you.

YOU DRAW THE CURTAIN

The night breaks into
a skirmish of flowers.

FORGIVENESS

I carry it
like a paper-pressed rose,
like an old stamp,
like a ticket stub
to a forgotten show.

Whenever I hold it
I am careful
that it does not fall
to pieces in my hands.

One day
you might ask for it.

THE LAST TIME I SAW YOU

I woke you up
to say a little goodbye.

You were half-asleep.

I kissed you
and left.

I don't remember
what you had murmured,
it could have been 'Are you sure?'
I was leaving very early.
The sun had not risen yet.

I don't remember my reply.

You were half-naked.
I kissed you
and left.

Imagine the first door
in the world that was knocked.

Imagine the feeling
of someone sitting inside

surprised by a small door
at last animate with arrival.

If I knew this was the last time,
what would I have said
how long would I have waited
what crumbs would I have left.

Keeping all those possible
sentences in my arms, I leave

then on and then on, to be
perpetually surprised by this morning,
by the simplicity of the going.

I don't remember
the colour of that fateful sky
as I climbed down your steps.

I decide to walk back to mine
only four kilometres away.

The morning held fast.

The city
was folding inwards.

Hardly anyone out
in the neighbourhood

no walkers, no car cleaners,
no women rushing to keep
the morning rituals of other people,

only a grey stillness,
quietly spreading.

The month of the sudden,
long lockdown.

I walked down not knowing
it was the last time

sentences still falling
from my arms – each one
a possibility this city could
not realize.

I walk. There is no catch
in the promise of this morning,
holding fast to a growing quiet.

I leave behind all the hours
we could have spent,
all the corners we could have
hushed into signs.

I reach the ring road.

As I cross into my neighbourhood
I see a long, quiet file of people
heading towards the river
and then – from the foot overbridge,

it is visible – outwards, and then
outwards

people, leaving the city
in a slow, deliberate step.

I see them from afar, keep walking
– the slowness is key, they
know the enormity of
the task at hand.

At one point, I cut across
their file. They have no business
with those whose homes are near.
They keep walking. The same slow
stride of a final pledge.

Each promise is broken.
Each hand is taken back.

They keep walking.

The grey asphalt is slowly
slowly shaken black.

They keep walking.

I reach my side of the road
and, for once, look back.

They keep walking.

They are going away,
suddenly unhomed,
their steps making
the shape of a large
abandonment.

Imagine the first city
in the world that was deserted.

Imagine the sounds
that the exiles took away with them.

That city will always live
in the crumbs of those silences.

'We've been abandoned
in the middle of nowhere,'
a man says to the camera,
expecting the world,
expecting nothing.

Does a thing change
when you see it for the last time.
Does it stop answering, already,
once it is behind your back.

I am near my home.
The tree is losing its sap.
The city is losing its people.
Each branch is being sapped.

The hours we could have spent
now lie indifferent
in the nearness
of our homes.

I reach. Already, behind
my back, a future has stopped answering.

As I climb to my floor,
you are already becoming the shape
that cannot be touched, a breach
in the grey distance

you are already
attenuating the stories
that could be told, now
each one ends
in the middle
of nowhere.

This city is becoming
a thing that no one
will recognize.

Each step is irreversible,
no crumbs to lay behind
one's final going.

'If we abandon this damned
city, it will starve,' a man says
to the camera.

The city is starving of its people.

They are far now,
too far, already across the river.

You are far now, too far
without me knowing
the breadth of this morning's
capacity to empty everything.

I open my door
and enter – in a quick, unguarded step –
a new abandonment.

MEMORY

A passing river writes a valley.

WHEN

Begum Akhtar sang her last song
Lata hummed her last tune
Shahid wrote his last line
Shakir inked her last noon

What signs had fallen on those
days, what omens lay unseen,
the world was ending in a million
ways from all that could have been

NIGHT

مینہ اس کے اندر رات ٹوٹ کے برسا تھا
मेह उसके अंदर रात टूटके बरसा था
All night, the rain poured inside him
Intizar Hussain

I return home to find
I left the bedroom window open.

A pigeon's come and gone
leaving a feather on the desk.

I pick it up from against
a thin hint of dust. It leaves
its feather shape behind.

I look at it for a second.

Then slip it inside
Intizar Hussain's *Basti*
on the page where
the night-rain is still falling
and Bee-Amma cannot sleep.

I close the book
and turn back.

Everywhere I look
in the room, someone
has come and gone.

The air is animal with their shapes.

I leave the window open,
come and sit on the bed.

Some nights
this city lives in the toenails
of the Aravallis

on others, it dances
on the hair-ends of those hills.

CLOUDS GATHER

burst

you
bring rain
in as footprints

into my home.

THE KITCHEN WINDOW

inside
dicing ginger
the mahak laps up
my fingers
a tendril rage
climbing

outside
the sudden
headlight of a bike

rain's falling cage
shining

ON DAY SIXTEEN OF LEARNING ITALIAN

we are finally
taught the words
for *yours* and *mine*.

Il tuo.
Il mio.

Possession.

It is the first lesson
in which I score decently
in the first try.

To abruptly
cut the sky into yours
and mine, and call it
a fair distribution.

The lesson has been older
than these weeks.

It will really end
when I can say
– without the tongue
drying in my mouth –
'The part of you
that is fiction
is mine.'

AS TADOLINI, THE SCULPTOR FROM ROME, FINISHES THE STATUE OF BEGUM SAMRU, IT SPEAKS

imparting him seven distinct visions.

1. A sarus crane, its feet disappearing in the wetland,
   wings stretched to each edge of Bharatpur, looks straight at me,
   its neck, reddened with ambition, its eyes carrara.

2. In the Qila's forlorn evening, Shah-e-Alam becomes the
   verses he composes, walks slowly, the twilight falls against the
   makrana, I see the old man become almost his 'shabnam
   ka araq'.

3. One morning, I see from my window, that the spires of my
   Church – now stalagmiting the Sardhana sky – finally have
   their crosses. In the distance, the new finials are blades of
   elephant grass.

4. One night, when no one is looking, I step out of my home,
   sit on the last step, eight Palladian pillars conspiring above me,
   I look on at the crenellated Lahori Gate, and I wonder, and
   I wonder.

5. How Sumru ki Begum is Commander-in-Chief is Nautch Girl
   of Chawri Bazaar is Zeb-un-Nissa is Farzand-i-Azizi is Beloved
   Daughter in Christ is Umdat-al-Arakin is Her Highness is also
   Farzana.

6. Is chained to a gun carriage. I see only the ground beneath, my undressed wound burning in the sun, clotting with dust, I wait for the water Amina will bring me at night. I must live. I must live.

7. Since once, on an elephant, leaving Ochterlony's, I began for home, the Qila's red on my shoulder, the onion domes of the Masjid far, I suddenly found, written in the serried sky, my name in cirrus.

with thanks to and for Julia Keay

BEHIND LAL QILA

the river
spills on to the road
in giant knots
of fog.

Which God was born
today

who won't let me see
ten hands ahead

ten hands behind.
A breath of water

fills up the space
I have just left.

We are each someone
whom someone else
can let go of.

I drive, very slowly,
into the colour
of pearls.

In the place
I leave behind
he must now pin
an ocean in air.

ON ONE OF THOSE LONG WALKS

I find myself again in your neighbourhood.

You no longer live there
but I still prepare for chance.

The front camera shows
the hair is all right. The belt buckle,
I pull it back on to the belly
from where it had slipped,
and give the sneakers
a quick rub-down
on the calves.

Now, from a distance, every person
of your approximate height
is you

and everyone who is wearing blue

and everyone who's passing by
with a look (that you'd perfected)
of both the hunted
and the hound.

Each step, as I near your street,
becomes a game of lost and found.

I keep walking. I keep walking.

All the people in the world
keep turning out to be not you.

LISTENING TO AN EVENING OF EUNICE DE SOUZA TRIBUTES

In her last years,
Gieve says, Eunice learnt first aid
from a vet and would treat the wounds
of the local strays.

After a while, dogs
she didn't know, from all over
Vakola, would come find her
on her street, turn around,
show her their wounds.

Once, her compound regular
brought a stranger to her door
for urgent treatment.

I imagine the poet
– those speaking of her
call her 'grande dame', formidable',
even 'charring' – surrounded
by dogs and parrots in the end.

Opening her apartment door
to find those who need healing.

I go to my bookshelf,
start looking up and down the spines
like the dogs of Vakola.

with thanks to Gieve Patel

LOOKING AT TWO PHOTOGRAPHS OF MUMBAI THAT INAYAT SENT

one clicked in the daytime, one at night

What changes?

At night-time
the lights are man-made.

They don't compare
with the arrangement
we have with the sun
(not even close)

it's like lighting a firecracker
next to a star

but room by room
each square of light
in the buildings across
from her own

someone has set fire to
their day

someone has
incinerated their wishes,
their plans, taken every thing
in their hands and put
a match to it

each window
now lit by the embers
of their catastrophe

that would outdo
each sun in this galaxy.

ANAPHORA

The past is mercury
on the tongue.

The past is rattle
snake.

The past is cube root
of a wish.

The past is what you make
while cloud-spotting.

The past is our wounds'
slow clotting.

The past is Luke
Chapter 23, Verse 34.

The past is a closing
door.

The past is buried
alive, looking to avenge.

The past has not
won yet.

The past is a night-long
body count.

The past
is not done yet.

HANDS

which otherwise
on a whim, have
hid the sun

which have held
the finial of the Taj Mahal
between forefinger and thumb

which have tapped
Ashokan pillars on their heads,
ruffled their hair

or saved the tower
from keeling over in Pisa

played the steel wires
of the Sea Link like
ukulele strings

and more such

now flounder
without your touch

FIRST KISS

Why I had to
close my mouth
on yours

like a hatchling
expecting food

having waited
having waited
so long

I thought
everything
that came from
inside you
would help me live

THE NAPE OF HIS NECK

is a coven of witches
a honeycomb of sweat

a slow burn
a connivery

Cleopatra's urn
cut in ivory

bird of prey
death's door

a quilt of cannabis
coup de grâce

locus mirabilis
looking glass

a dying wish
crushed like quartz

AND WHEN HE WAS ABOUT TO SAY

something big like 'I love you'
or 'I am sorry', I turned the English
audio off and heard him say the words
in a language I did not know.

It sounded like it had always sounded.
The same goosebumps on my arms.
The same drying of my mouth.
The same incapacity of replying.

Maybe the claim of love is always
made in a language we do not know
– in the same language in which we
are then left to ask for forgiveness.

EUNICE DE SOUZA HEARS MY AGONIES

He has gone,
I complain.

I don't know how
I will survive it this time.

He was so pretty,
I assure her.

At thirty-five,
one asks for certainties,
right?

She listens, kindly,
an eye on the clock
senses danger.

In the end, she assures me,
one prefers
a good bowel movement
over love.

A QUARREL CAN END IN TWO WAYS

He'll talk, you'll talk,
he'll explain, then you'll explain,
then the gods will sit in judgement
and finally it will rain
reconciliation (or one of its
many synonyms).

Or

After hours of silence
he will message 'Goodnight Nunnu'.

There are two kinds of light
at work always.

One: The sun emits so much
that it reaches Saturn.

Two: A firefly
makes a whole rainforest talk.

HAIKU ON A TWO-WHEELER

Copernicus Marg –
he rode slowly under a
quarrel of branches.

HAIKU

for Naaz

Meena Kumari
picks her radif – *tanha*.
A moonquake.

BAD DATE HAIKU

Noisy cafe. We
attempt conversation.
Oil in water.

I SEE REELS

in which kids
spell out a word
letter by letter, and when
asked to put it together
say something else entirely.

In one, a girl reads
P, A, R, L, E, G, very, very
confidently, and says 'biscuit'.

In another, a boy reads
each letter, C, H, A, M, P, I, O, N
printed on his leg and says 'pajama'.

How wonderful
to make one word spell another.
A right sort of game.

That night, in my sleep
I spell out W, H, E, R, E
and take your name.

IF SOMETHING TAKES ME DOWN THESE DAYS

I no longer talk myself out of it.

I have started relying on the slow dissolve of time.

The next day the pinch is (infinitesimally) thinner.

The day after, it is lighter by the weight of light.

It goes like the candle goes into flame, slowly.

This is the mathematics of belief in the hours.

The stone-polisher of time works on every marble of grief.

You hold out the uncut diamond of what you said.

I take it in my palm and dip it in the acid of passing years.

ON A FLIGHT FROM BENGALURU TO DELHI WHILE A CRICKET MATCH IS BEING PLAYED 37,000 FEET BELOW BETWEEN INDIA AND PAKISTAN

Half an hour into the flight
the air hostess announces she has
managed to dig out the score
– 'since a lot of you asked' –
'Pakistan has made 59 runs for two wickets.'

Heated debates
spring like cabbage clumps
on each row.

A bunch of dudes on the 22s
make bold mid-air predictions
with edgy fist bumps.

A crop of nerves grow
as if the AC vent has leaked
into the plane, a mixture
of oxygen and hypertension.

What is this country
that at the mere mention of
our neighbour's name
grows new limbs of zeal.

What is this wedge
between them
that slices even the sky.

Cricket alone does not explain it.

The name of that country, that
like a chant, pendulums
through the rows.

In whose shadow
our love for our own
grows.

That country is the name
of a strange need, a weird force
we don't explain to ourselves,
a match made in heaven – a brutal
necessity of another people
to make one's own.

Twins gone rogue.
Lonely clones.
Two countries.
Two matchsticks.

That country we play a match with
that country we will match with
that country 'who's no match'
that country we were hatched with.

READING RILKE'S 'LOVE SONG' IN GERMAN

without knowing the language

I cut into the new song
in a riot of emphasis and sputum.

Softness, if there was any,
leaves the notes as lips practise
the riddle of umlauts.

A mouth unused to the sounds
of the Danube is trying
the dubious vowels
with two dots.

Speaking a language without knowing it
is also a name for love.

The desire to know, kneeling
before the difficult consonants
now rain-drenched in my throat.

The tongue cedes to other,
uninhabitable streets, finds
its way without asking for directions.

The incisors finally sever
the song in two.

In one version,
I don't understand a thing.

In the other, everything that
comes out of my mouth takes your shape.

with thanks to Len Krisak

SOUNDS

in ascending order of decibels

the press of paper on paper
the click of the pen cap
the susurrus of leaves
the first attempt at a bark
    by a three-day-old pup
the thump of a falling book
the call of the guy hawking
    knives
the neighbour's car horn
the neighbours fighting
    over car parking
the low-flying domestic airline
the polisher working on marble
the banyan, older than the mutiny,
    falling in a storm
    its trunk exploding
    into a million mouths
your last words

VALUABLES

I sense
the first tremors.

Before rushing
down the stairs

I reach for
the envelope.

Your handwriting
crumpling in my grasp.

Long ago, you had asked
me to courier it.

I'd forgotten. It remained
in my bedside drawer since

always
at one arm's distance.

The quaking
of the earth

written
in your handwriting.

ANOTHER INVENTED MEMORY

near Bachhrawan

You sat down
in the soft crunch
of drying leaves.

We had gone off the road
till we found a clump of shisham trees
and decided to call it a forest.

A lake – the size of three fists –
began where your feet ended,
was cluttered with lotus leaves,
like so many open palms
trying to refuse the summer sun.

When I found that you'd forgotten
the water bottle in the car, I chose
to be petty and argued over the plural
of 'lotus' with unmerited zeal –
'lotuses' you said, I said 'loti'
and rhymed it with bow tie.

I forgot that sometimes
both of us could be wrong.

You ended my valiant attempt
at a fight with a smile
shaped like a shisham leaf.

The tree, above, finding itself
so alluded in your face, gifted your cheek
shifting sun-prints.

I RUN INTO A GHOST OF A PALAEOLITHIC DUDE AT THE RIDGE AND ASK HIM WHAT'S WHAT

Don't you feel lonely sometimes?

No, there are many more like me.

It is so cold here. Where do you sleep?

In the quartzite.

What do you eat?

The grains of the quartzite
and the leaves of the kikar.

Who do you tell your secrets to?

I draw them in the caves.

What does this circle mean?
It looks like a Raza painting.

I told others it was the sun.
What it really is, I won't tell you.

Do you ever step out of the ridge?

When the Siberian gulls
come in the winter, I go to
feed them at the Jamuna.

Will you come to my home for tea?

If you bring me jarul flowers.
I have none here.

Do you ever get tired of us?

No, some of you know
where the water is and
which branch is to be cut.

Do you know any songs?

Yes. It begins with 'we'
and is thousands of years old.

IF YOU HAVE EVER FELT UNLOVED OR UNWANTED

go to your spam folder.

There, Mrs Marsha Williams
tycoon from the Upper East Side
will be 'waiting for you to come
down and pick up your Bank Draft
of Four Million Dollars'.

She will tell you
she has not heard from you
in a long time, will be the right kind
of petulant.

There, Susan from the Bahamas
who opens with a 'cómo estás'
will be 'seeking in you an urgent partner'.
She wants to work together with you
'across the seven oceans' to make
'an unbeatable team'. She is everything
she seems.

There, Shirlee Patterson
with her Hollywood name
will have 'something very important
to discuss with you'.
Don't you want to discuss
'something very important'?

Or Miss Rachel Omer from Dubai
who will call you 'my dear'
which is, frankly, the sort
of thing all of us like to hear.

Like Dr (Mrs) Laura, who is confident
that you can help her out of the mess
she has landed herself in
during her vacation in Bali.
Only you can save her.

Or Miriam, who's Somali
– who thinks you're a braveheart –
and is so sure of your abilities to help her
escape her abductors in the Gulf of Aden.
She insists on a small transaction but
sees the superhero in you.

Or Mr Richard Wahl, who just had
the good fortune of winning $533M
in a lottery, has – imagine the scale
of his generosity – realized what no one
around you realizes, your inner & outer
paucity, and selects you to be among
the 'five random individuals' to donate
a significant part of his new-found bounty.

This *is* the luck world, the love world,
here you are Noah who will save mankind
from the flood, here, you're the perennial

stud, Majnu to all Lailas, Ranjha to all Heers,
a man of hundred abilities and no fears
and still the one who needs love, money,
kindness, friendship, a way ahead in the world.
Won't you stay here a while, soak in the glow
of this strange underworld, and hear the lies
only loved ones can tell, in this freakish corner
of our otherwise hell, where we know the waves
are stormy, so we enter this shell, enter this shell.

THE ABANDONED TRUCK ON THE WAY TO AGRA

has stood in this spot
for so long, an acacia
has grown within

the babool's thin trunk
– used to deserts –
makes a home in this giant's
fortunate desertion
climbs out of his belly.

An accident, years ago
took his face off
now thorns grow
from his steel-scrap throat.

Often, couples
from the nearby Basera Colony
enter his big wound
in search of some dark.

Once they are inside him
the capillaries
of their lust spread

disturbed only
by a colony
of bank mynas

which have returned
to this skeleton-shelter
after an evening of foraging.

They are breathing
in his injuries.

Each evening
under the weight
of a mad, relentless kiss
of the lovers, rushing against
the wristwatch
of the night

the giant sinks into the earth
by a tenth of a fingernail.

IT WAS THE SEASON OF

millipede suicides.

In every park
they'd crawl straight
into the mud paths
of the evening walkers

moving, all too slowly,
in and out of the sunspots
till a stray sneaker
crushed them.

After the hit-job
they already resembled
their fossils, flattened into a lesson.

Despite the carnage,
more kept coming.

Their bravado
reminded me of you.
In those years, when we thought
we could live, always,
in the small streak of the sun.

A thousand legs couldn't save them.

IN BHOGAL MARKET

I overheard her
scolding her child,
'Do not eat those seeds
or they will sprout like trees
from your belly.'

Parents say
the most terrifying things
to children shaking like leaves.

They pass on
– so proudly –
a rulebook of fears,
then quietly note the terror
in the child's eyes, of a sudden knowledge
thrust upon him, growing over years:
  the cliff he will fall from
  the old man who'll abduct him
  the inspector who will torture him
  the dog that will bite him to bone
  and blood, the ghost that'll destruct him

and when he grows to be
– as all of us must do –
a country of fears

true or untrue, he will read back
all his fallibilities to them:

the job he could not keep,
the nights he could not sleep,
the loves that fell apart,
he will find, in each way the world recedes
from him, his parents' part

he won't be kind, he won't stop
to think whether this resentment
is merited, will find no space
to consider their fears, the ones
that they inherited

instead, each day,
through the cuts, he will look at them
with the glaze-eyed arrogance
of a beggar

and offer them
the long, dark branch
growing, for years,
tearing his guts.

HOW RIVERS CROSS THEIR CITIES

Near a church in Karrada,
the Tigris takes a sharp turn
as if it doesn't want to
leave Baghdad.

The Lyari in Karachi
on the other hand, can't be
bothered to stay.

Through Delhi,
the Yamuna is a moral lesson
clear as day: *life is tough,*
first a trough, then a crest,
then a trough.

The Chenab,
knowing better, walks on stilts,
keeps a one-arm distance from Jhang.

The Ganga
covers Patna like a quilt.

The Gomti baby-bumps
through Lucknow.

And when it's about to leave,
the Adyar turns to take
a last look at Chennai.

As the Ravi
cold-presses Lahore's
burning cheek.

I AM WEARING AN OMEN

cut like solitaire on a ring.

I am reading thumbs
left in by photocopiers.

I am telling the city
I will need cradling.

I am asking ice caps
not to melt too soon.

I am memorizing
my world like elephants.

I am learning the roots
of *bereaved. To be robbed.*

I am building a shrine
to the saint of long distance.

I am being born again
a stray dog, loyal to strangers.

You were beautiful
like ground pepper.

Like a long neck
before slaughter.

You'd ask, 'Why can't you
stop the rain for me?'

You who crossed all rivers,
who singed even water.

WE SKIRT MINEFIELDS

every day.

Around the corners
of our rooms are memories
which we do not allow
to consume us in gulps

so the next day
can be brought, and the night.

We tiptoe
around the terrible things
those we love say to us.

We aren't able
to let them know
how even their love
can suddenly
reduce us.

It is difficult work
to build an estimation of yourself
over years, it is a cruel abacus
so easily decimated by a chance
thing your mother says

or what someone's promise
once, laid out for you, in neat furrows

finally holds back, becomes a line
you then never cross.

We shuffle back, then,
into things we'd been telling
ourselves, rely on precarious
(because self-made) courage.

One day, when we'd
let the afternoon remain
behind the curtain, you'd made me
stand up, made me hold
my hands behind my head,
took off all my clothes,
and did not leave
a single inch of my body
unkissed.

Hours must have passed
in that room held afloat only
by my breath. It was
a sort of anointing
into a new belief.

How will I outlive the trembling
promise of that gesture, how will I
outlive that long afternoon
and not repose trust in everyone
I have once loved. And how
will we not believe those who have,

assuredly, in ways, found means
to love us back, to share
with us however little
the yield of the season was.

How will I not expect
my mother, in all her limitations,
– the grounds she has walked,
the walls she has struck –
to still be capable of a love
that verges on the
miraculous.

Each conversation that we do
not have, I keep entrusting her
with so much benefit of doubt,
it must be unfair to anyone, to expect
so much understanding, so much
capacity to keep you in their eyes,
as you keep yourself in yours.

No one, not your lovers,
not your parents, not the chance
windows which open with friends
on some 'dew-starched' nights,
is to be held to that vetting,
to that cruel anvil.

We must hope
in others, we must let them

mistake us for the images
they have of us in the small vials
of their eyes.

We must be kind
to the little breaches that let them
begin to know us, that let them
build us anew, even if their
outlines do not toe ours.

We must be kind to the small days
we have with them,
to the small afternoons
when we thought we could ask
for the world, when we thought
everything we could want was held
in the traverse of their little hands.

WHEN YOU WENT

you left me a pebble.

Small, uncertain, grey.

I kept it in my pocket
and forgot about it.

Each day it grew in size,
till one day, it tugged.

I took it out, kept it on my desk,
played with it often while
reading a book.

That was years ago.

Over time, it became
too big for my hands.
And grew veins
like stretchmarks.
I hid it then in the almirah.

Last year when I saw it
tucked behind old clothes,
I couldn't lift it.

I rolled it out, heavy, grumbling
like a gas cylinder, pushed it
to the balcony, and let it remain.

It keeps growing
with the invisible speed of plants.

Men make promises.

It grows limbs.

Men take my word.

It reaches for the night sky.

Men listen. Impatient,
discovering things about their lovers.

One day
it will eclipse all the stars.

JLN STADIUM FROM MY TERRACE

The Barapullah cars
jump off, one by one, into
the guldaudi of light.

A MONSOON EVENING

Above me,
the bats, cartilaged
against a Lutyens blue,
set off.

The jamun below
crushed on the asphalt
haemorrhages purple.

Days without you
offer promise
– raindrops
on an anthill.

THE NIGHT WRAPS UP

like a wedding band
instruments hung up
in old knapsacks,
trumpets, trombones
walking back, quietly
in the cold fog, their
spell over, on bone-
tired familiar shoulders.

PASSING BY

I see a strange tree
laden with clay pots.

At Matka Peer, when
your wish comes true

you fill jaggery, milk and
gram in plain earthenware

and offer it, first, at the feet
of the Qalandar.

Passing by, others see the
ecstatic weight the tree bears –

a tree of fulfilled wishes
a tree of answered prayers.

THE CREMATION GROUND

near my home
has decided to paint
doves on its outer wall.

White feathers
against a deep blue,
each flying off
in a different direction.

If you were to
extrapolate their lines
of flight, they'd
go to all the cities
you know.

Weeks ago
I met a photographer,
who in his book
traced the last days
of his dying father.

In its last pages
the images were
deliberately blurred
and the death itself
was withheld
from us.

Instead, several stills
of a hospital waiting room,
crowded in the day,
slowly thinning as the last
pages turn, till, in the last shot,
the room was bare, the evening
had emptied it entirely
of people.

And I am thinking
both these gestures
are not euphemisms
– the doves on the wall
and the waiting room –
they do not shy away from
the brutal fact of death,
they do not seek
to thin its import.

A son gifts dignity
to a dying father
– by turning away
from the face
of illness, just as
it begins its irreversible
crash into the body –
he takes the camera,

quietly, to another room
('to save you as you were'
another poet had once said).

The painter,
commissioned to redo
the crematorium wall,
knows – in that act
of limning the feathers,
one by one – that
when people go,
when they fly off
in those eccentric directions
that we cannot track,
they empty everything
we know, all the cities
we ever walked in,
all the towns to which
we'll go.

His doves (not red herrings)
are not polite synonyms
for the barefaced finality
of death, they are, instead,
its recompense.
They conjure a possibility,
that each of us might,

even in the final act of going,
somehow, against the iron fact,
imagine the skies,
imagine a flight.

for Adil Hasan
and the painter(s) whose name(s)
I do not know

WHAT WE DID NOT MAKE WAS

our own *bedroom farce*. That
next step never came. You
did not, for instance, mark
indelibly a preferred side of
the bed, did not every night
oil your slowly thinning hair,
or fill up two water bottles to
keep near, on the side table. I
did not have to get used to a
dim red light bulb, or a slow
debate on the day just past, I
did not have to separate our
medicines into little tupper
boxes, winding down for the
night, or speak about a very
infuriating colleague. We left
each other before any dailiness
could set in, each time we met
was still somehow an event.
We protected ourselves from
rituals in the fear of the other
leaving. Now I lie under the
double quilt, dividing night
chores. It's the turn of your
memory to switch off the light.

with thanks to Alan Ayckbourn

I OFTEN GO TO THAT PILGRIMAGE SPOT IN MY CITY

where you and I sat once
and said those words

(I won't repeat them
here but you know
that evening).

Often when a day
slips out of my hand,
I go sit there.

It was cold today –
that metro-station granite.

Around it,
they have now
planted champa trees.

Their shade doubles up
as a sanctorum.

I sat there for an hour.

People thought I was waiting
for someone.

People were right.

Everyone on a pilgrimage
is waiting for someone

for a small god
to turn suddenly kind

to step out of his home
and will a flower
to drop into our laps.

No one suspects
this guy sitting against the stone
is praying for the day
to solve itself

is taking the snow-bitten air
in his hand and turning it
into a god

that even his empty hands
are an offering.

Look how the distance
is turning everything we touched
into a blessing.

I take this empty space
and give it an origin myth.

In this story
each one of us
– in the end –
turns into branches
bursting into
champa.

THE PHOTOGRAPH, NOW UNTRACEABLE

at Safdarjung Tomb

If you were to count the
number of inlaid flowers

in each panel, you would
run out of gemstones.

I can see mud-coloured
irises, sky-blue sunflowers

and two tangerine roses
arranged like tail feathers.

Whose idea was it to give
wrong colours to the flowers?

We stand under this rain of
muqarnas, arched in their lie.

The sandstone makes a last
try to hold on to the past.

My hand, uncertain on your
shoulder, is opening outwards

as if already offering its palm
to be read by unkind strangers.

and now when my days blacken like metal and the bones
inside my chest triple I bend in places I did not know
were secret stashes of dignity I find two skies made
only of fear and one made of memory someone
hands me a map like a child I begin to find
my room I live these days like a falling
every hour a word disappears and
anchors rust in mariana trench
things go away from me like
people when I sit up on
my bed late nights it
is as if language
has not been
invented
yet

I STEP OUT OF GRIEF

into a Szymborska poem.
into a night of gentle ribbing.
into the remaining whisper of a promise.
into Rahim talking of cucumbers.
into perfect forgetfulness.
into the etymology of *desideratum*.
into a floating terrace.
into the monsoon of his arms.
into a translation of *loon main balaiyyan.*
into an eleventh-century fort
  overgrown with colonies of lantana.
into Rahim talking of needles.
into a dream of my first swimming teacher.
into the bottom of Naomi Shihab Nye's shoes
  to find 'the poems that had been hiding
    in the eyes of skunks for centuries'.
into the obverse side of sandpaper
  that carries its softness.
into proofs of the softness of this igneous world.
into Rahim talking of pearls.
into this banana peel of a day.
into a smile made in Khatauli.
into the pathway of Siberian seagulls
  waylaid by the false promise of the Yamuna.
into the name of my great-grandmother
  who came from Bhalwaal.
into the peonies left outside
  Winehouse's apartment.

into the bet each of us makes with October.
into Rahim talking of threads and knots.
into the tenacity of the knots of quartzite.
into the neck of this God.
into the sudden etymology of *seer*
  on Omvedt's page.
into a single movement of Chaur Sahib,
  each of its strands made of worship.
into Rahim insisting on animating
  every object in the world,
    turning out their mutinous lies.
into this night,
  into its slow sapphire skies.
into what Satnam once told Amandeep,
  pushing him from behind, 'Just a little rain.
    You are not made of salt.'
into the resilient red on the forehead
  of the sandhill crane.
into not being made of salt.
into the arms of falling rain.

AFTER EACH STORM

the calm
of

Ik Onkar Satnam

After each scar
the balm
of

Ik Onkar Satnam

After each word
the psalm
of

Ik Onkar Satnam

उस पर लदा बरसों का कबाड़ रेत रेत गिरने लगे।
सरक जाए, लुढ़क जाए, वो आज़ाद होती जाए,
वो छोटी होती जाए, वो हल्की होती जाए।
इतनी हल्की कि वो रेत के भीतर से उठने लगे।
जैसे समाधि से। रेत के कण के संग उड़ने लगे।
उसके मुँह से सीटी के स्वर निकलें, अनजान दुनिया
में लहराते, हवा को हवा से जोड़ते।

GEETANJALI SHREE

Years of dreck turn to sand and begin to fall away.
Let her slip, tumble; she will be freed, she will
keep shrinking, growing lighter. So light,
she'll start to rise from the sand. As from a tomb.
As from a trance. As from a tomb-like trance.
She will begin to fly with the particles of sand.
A whistling sound will emerge from her mouth;
it will tremble in an unfamiliar world, binding air to air.

tr. DAISY ROCKWELL

ACKNOWLEDGEMENTS

Rahul Soni's and Sohini Basak's perceptive editorial comments on this manuscript have been invaluable.

Kanishka Gupta is a literary agent of one's dreams.

These years have been spent in a limbo. Unable to distinguish the going forward from the slipping backwards, the days were allowed what the days did. Now a rent has appeared in the sky, slowly but surely. Several people, in ways they do and do not know, have carried me along the way.

Vikramaditya Sahai is my most precious daily-phone-call-and-midnight-wordle buddy. Their thoughts shift mine.

Aditi Rao has been my closest confidante for years and I trust no one's advice more while editing a poem.

Anannya Dasgupta is Pan-India Writing Beyoncé and my gold standard for most things writing. I value her incredible friendship and generosity of spirit.

Anusha Hariharan always lends her ears all the way from 'North Hill'.

Vebhuti Duggal made my former workplace liveable.

Dhrubo Jyoti offers joy and courage in astounding measure.

Natasha Narwal is full of fellow-feeling.

Sonal Sharma and Dhiren Borisa's meme-sharing is legendary.

Yuvraj rushed me to the Emergency when I broke my arm. Vikram took over from him and proved to be the patron saint of the dislocated.

Grief is not resolved in a miraculous breakthrough but in the slow undergrowth of the ordinary. These people have made up my ordinary.

G is now so far away in the past that thanking him seems like betraying some sort of a code. But he made so much possible in those days that even a great store of thankfulness will not be amiss.

REFERENCES

Epigraphs and quotations in this book have been taken from Ruth Padel's *Beethoven Variations: Poems on a Life* (Knopf, 2021), Krishna Sobti's *Dilo-Danish* (Rajkamal Prakashan, 2018), John Keats' 'On the Grasshopper and Cricket' (Poetry Foundation), Haseena Moin's *Ankahi* (PTV, 1982), Intizar's Hussain's *Basti* (Radhakrishna Paperbacks, 2019 [1982]), Geetanjali Shree's *Ret Samadhi* (Rajkamal Prakashan, 2022) and its translation by Daisy Rockwell as *Tomb of Sand* (Penguin, 2022) and Louise Glück's *Faithful and Virtuous Night* (Farrar, Straus and Giroux, 2015).

ABOUT THE AUTHOR

AKHIL KATYAL is a writer, translator and scholar. He has published three books of poems: *Like Blood on the Bitten Tongue: Delhi Poems* (2020), *How Many Countries Does the Indus Cross* (2018) and *Night Charge Extra* (2015). He was a 2016 International Writing Fellow at the University of Iowa International Writing Program and was awarded the Vijay Nambisan Poetry Fellowship in 2021. He translated Ravish Kumar's *Ishq Mein Shahar Hona* as *A City Happens in Love* (2018). In 2020, he co-edited *The World That Belongs to Us: An Anthology of Queer Poetry from South Asia*. His work has appeared in several pivotal anthologies, including *The Penguin Book of Indian Poets* edited by Jeet Thayil. He is the Associate Professor of Literature at BITS Law in Mumbai.

HarperCollins *Publishers* India

At HarperCollins India, we believe in telling the best stories and finding the widest readership for our books in every format possible. We started publishing in 1992; a great deal has changed since then, but what has remained constant is the passion with which our authors write their books, the love with which readers receive them, and the sheer joy and excitement that we as publishers feel in being a part of the publishing process.

Over the years, we've had the pleasure of publishing some of the finest writing from the subcontinent and around the world, including several award-winning titles and some of the biggest bestsellers in India's publishing history. But nothing has meant more to us than the fact that millions of people have read the books we published, and that somewhere, a book of ours might have made a difference.

As we look to the future, we go back to that one word—a word which has been a driving force for us all these years.

Read.